MAXIMUM ACHIEVEMENT

THE BRIAN TRACY STORY

Published by Impact Publishing®, Orlando, FL.

Impact Publishing® is a registered trademark.

Printed in the United States of America.

ISBN: 978-1-7334176-1-7
LCCN: 2019912087

The opinions expressed by the individuals in this book are not endorsed by Impact Publishing® and are the sole responsibility of the individual rendering the opinion. Trademarks and licensed images are the property of the rights holder and some of the images are used under license.

Most Impact Publishing® titles are available at special quantity discounts for bulk purchases for sales promotions, premiums, fundraising, and educational use. Special versions or book excerpts can also be created to fit specific needs.

For more information, please write:
Impact Publishing®
520 N. Orlando Ave, #2
Winter Park, FL 32789
or call 1.877.261.4930

A FILM BY
Nick Nanton

EXECUTIVE PRODUCERS
JW DICKS
Nick Nanton

EXECUTIVE PRODUCERS
Kevin Hodes
Brian Douglas
Clay Dugas
Richard Tyler
West Seegmiller

"**OUR NEXT TRAINER HAS BEEN ONE OF THE TOP BUSINESS AND PERSONAL SUCCESS SPEAKERS IN THE ENTIRE WORLD.** HE'S GIVEN TALKS AND SEMINARS IN EVERY MAJOR CITY IN THE UNITED STATES AND CANADA AND OVER 45 DIFFERENT COUNTRIES. EACH YEAR HE SPEAKS TO OVER A QUARTER MILLION PEOPLE, ALMOST HALF A BILLION DOLLARS IN SALES AND PRODUCTS ALONE. HE HAS WRITTEN 45 BOOKS. I AM THRILLED TO HAVE WITH US, MR. BRIAN TRACY."

EXECUTIVE PRODUCERS
KEVIN HODES
BRIAN DOUGLAS
CLAY DUGAS
RICHARD TYLER
WEST SEEGMILLER

PRODUCERS
KEN COURTRIGHT
KERRI COURTRIGHT
MATTHEW CRAVEY
TAMARA MAGALOTTI
ALAN BONNER
BARRY GOLDWATER

PRODUCERS
FAI CHAN
VICTOR EKE-SPIFF
GARY MARRIAGE
EDWARD FITZGERALD
MUTHU G. MUDALIAR

STORY PRODUCER
Emily Hache

EDITOR
Nick Ruff

ASSISTANT EDITOR
Alyson Clancy

DIRECTOR OF PHOTOGRAPHY
RAMY ROMANY

ADDITIONAL CINEMATOGRAPHY
CARLO ALBERTO ORECCHIA
ROB HACHE
PARKER YATES
MARCO TOMASELLI

PRODUCTION ASSISTANT
KATIE TSCHOPP

BRIAN TRACY

LET ME BEGIN BY SAYING WE ARE LIVING AT THE VERY BEST TIME IN ALL OF HUMAN HISTORY.

I am an economist by avocation. I read. I keep current with what's going on in the world. I've traveled in 90 countries and I can tell you that North America is the most booming, single place in the world today. There are more opportunities, more possibilities, for more people today than have ever existed in any other country, at any other time in human history. And you are at the front of the line to take advantage of them. And our job today, our job in this conference, is to give you ideas that you can use to take full advantage of this.

INTERVIEWER You wrote the book, *Eat That Frog!* Phenomenal book.

INTERVIEWER (CONTINUES) What was the concept behind *Eat That Frog!* and one or two key time management lessons we can take away, sir?

BRIAN TRACY I'll give you a couple of concepts...

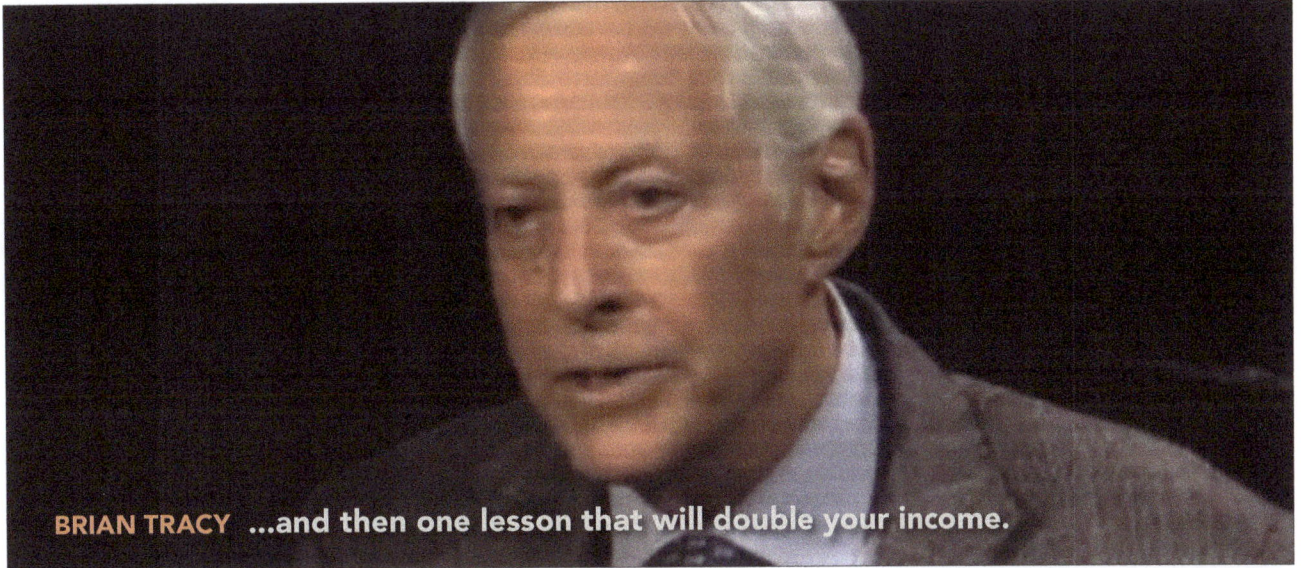

BRIAN TRACY ...and then one lesson that will double your income.

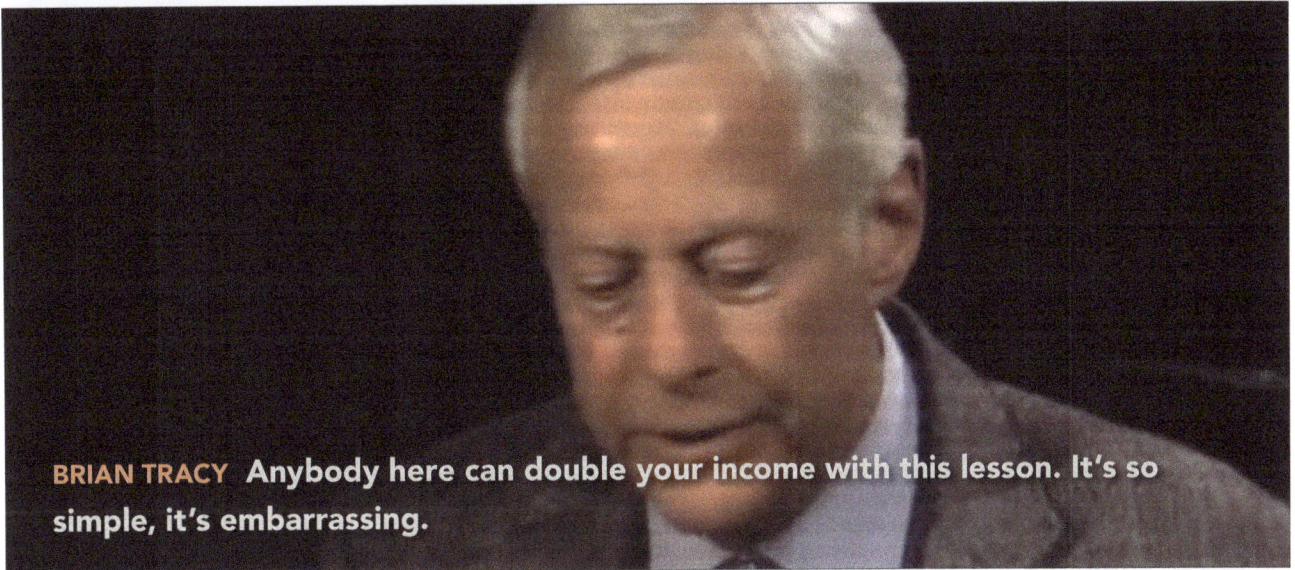

BRIAN TRACY Anybody here can double your income with this lesson. It's so simple, it's embarrassing.

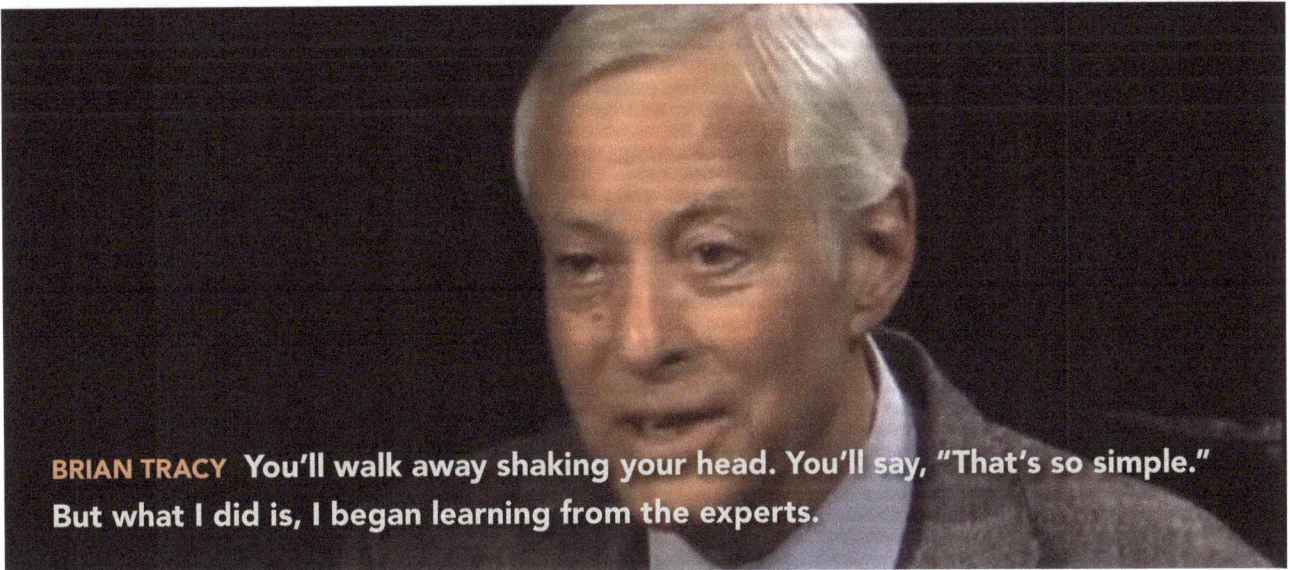

BRIAN TRACY You'll walk away shaking your head. You'll say, "That's so simple." But what I did is, I began learning from the experts.

BRIAN TRACY

OVER THE YEARS, I BEGAN TO STUDY THE SUBJECT OF SUCCESS. AND I HAD ONE SIMPLE IDEA THAT CAME UPON ME IN MY LATE TEENS AND I THINK IT WAS THE MOST IMPORTANT IDEA THAT I'VE EVER HAD. AND IT WAS SIMPLY THIS, THAT IF YOU STUDY SUCCESSFUL PEOPLE AND YOU DO WHAT THEY DO, YOU'LL BE MORE SUCCESSFUL.

DIRECTED
NICK NANTON

MAXIMUM ACHIEVEMENT
THE BRIAN TRACY STORY

"

I love Brian Tracy. I've known Brian for probably 30 or 40 years. I've followed his work from the time I was probably in my 30s. And Brian has this unbridled enthusiasm for life, this belief that anybody can do anything. He is someone who has studied and read probably more books than I have and I've read 3,000 books. He's so articulate and so well thought, so considered, so understanding of what he's teaching that when he teaches it, you get it."

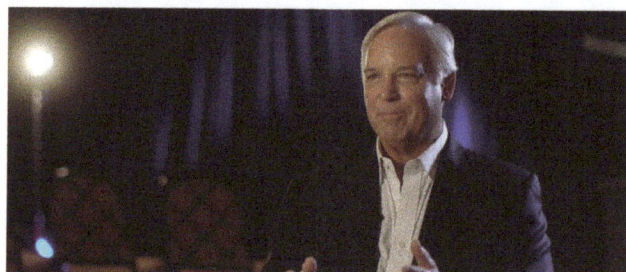

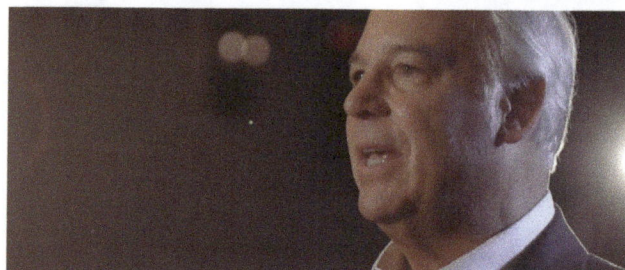

MATT CRAVEY
COMMERCIAL REAL ESTATE BROKER
CORPUS CHRISTI, TX

"

Back in the 80s, when things were not going real well for me and I was really second guessing myself as to what was the problem, why I wasn't doing better, and of course the economy was doing bad. About that time, Nightingale-Conant sends a direct mail piece and it's promoting Brian Tracy. I never heard of Brian Tracy."

ALAN BONNER
ENTREPRENEUR
BRIGHTONS, SCOTLAND

"

It might be 30 years ago or more probably, that I'm growing up listening to Brian Tracy. And the thing that ran around my head for decades was, 'If it's up to me, it has to be.' Or, 'If it has to be, it's up to me.'"

RAHO BORNHORST
SPIRITUAL TEACHER
GERMANY

"

Brian really has it. He's got something, all the bullet points and everything is valuable. In Germany he's famous now for being the person with the most valuable information per minute. And he got awards for that."

VICTOR EKE-SPIFF
TRANSFORMATIONAL LIFE COACH
PORT HARCOURT, NIGERIA

"

My wife was going into business and then I looked around and I thought to myself that I had to be careful with her, otherwise I would lose a lot of money because she never had any training in business and yet she wanted to go into business full time. So I decided to enroll in Brian Tracy University. So, that let me learn something and know a little more about business so I could give that kind of support to my wife. And honestly I must tell you that I'm not too sure now, who really needed this training—whether my wife or myself."

"HELLO, I'M BRIAN TRACY.
REPEAT AFTER ME"

"I AM RESPONSIBLE."

"I LIKE MYSELF."

RICHARD TYLER
SALES TRAINER & MANAGEMENT CONSULTANT
HOUSTON, TX

"

These are timeless philosophies.
I think the greatness of any
country, certainly I think the
greatness of America and
other places that have been
successful in the world, is how
its people rise to success."

Scene Secrets of Self-made Millionaires, 2005

BRIAN TRACY

Now, some of you will say, "Well, I started off without any money and I don't have any money now." Well, join the crowd. Nobody's got any money. Most people are broke up into their 40s and 50s.

"So if you're broke today, you're just one of the gang."

The only question is do you stay there, and the answer is no. In the last two years, the number of millionaires has jumped 33%. It's jumped to 8.2 million millionaires.

SAN DIEGO

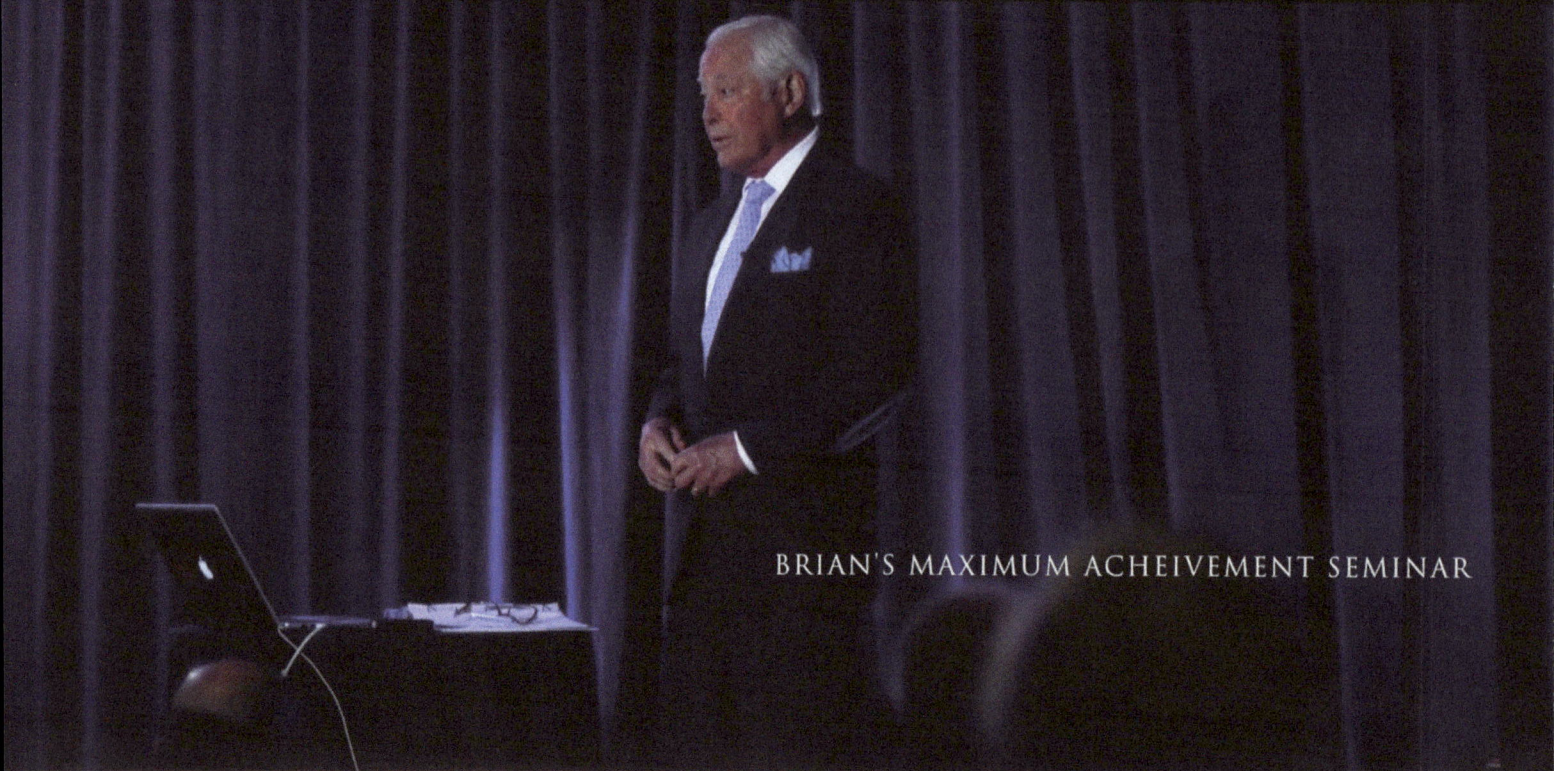

BRIAN'S MAXIMUM ACHEIVEMENT SEMINAR

Scene: Brian speaking to audience

BRIAN TRACY

Good morning and thank you for being here. Many years ago, coming from a poor family with no money and no hope and not graduated from high school, I started out to see the world. I'd read all kinds of books and articles about travelers and adventurers when I was a teenager, and spending a lot of time alone, and I didn't learn until later that what I was doing was I was programming my mind to want to be like the people I read about. So, when I hit the age of 18 I wanted to travel. By the time I finished traveling, I'd been to more than 120 countries! I learned French, German, Spanish and some other languages, in part. I have worked and spoken in 77 countries, and my materials are translated into 42 languages.

But it all started with this desire to travel. I didn't have any money, so I got an old car and I drove it across the country and left it at the docks in Montreal. I got job on a ship working my way across to England. I met up with a couple of my friends from high school

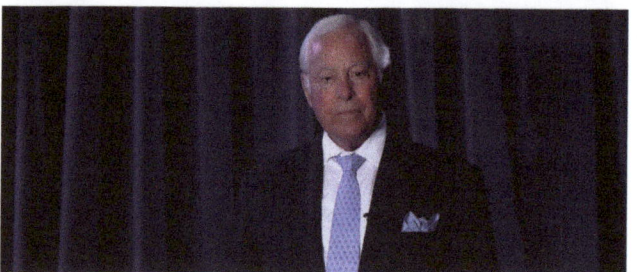

"...IT ALL STARTED WITH THIS DESIRE TO TRAVEL."

and we rode bicycles across Europe to Gibraltar. It was one of the most terrible, awful experiences of human life.

In France, when you are riding bicycles, all the hills are uphill and the wind is always in your face. And by the way, that's the way life seems to be when you start anything new. All the hills are uphill and wind is always in your face. We got to Gibraltar and we said, "The heck with this." So we wrote to everybody that we knew and we begged them on bended knee to send us money.

Our friends sent us some dribs and drabs of money and finally we had enough to buy an old Land Rover. We packed our stuff in, we crossed across the Straits of Gibraltar to Tangier and from Tangier we worked ourselves across and down the Sahara Desert and across Africa and finally ended up some months later in Johannesburg.

🎬 **Scene** Brian speaking to audience

Goals have played a central role in my life. Up to the age of 23 or 24, I didn't know

29

anything about goals. I thought they were things that took place in sports. It's not that I had not set and achieved goals, but I didn't really understand what they were. They were more accidental and more survival-based than deliberate.

Scene: Brian speaking to audience

When I was growing up, my father was never regularly employed. He went from job to job. He was a little bit lazy. He stayed at home a lot and watched television all day, in the early days of television when there was nothing on. Unfortunately he'd had a bad upbringing, so he just criticized me and the other kids all the time. Nothing we ever did was right. I think the first compliment I got from my parents was when I was 15 years old and I still remember it. The car was crossing a bridge and I still remember, like a flash of a photograph, that first compliment, the first positive statement when I was 15.

We never had enough money. I used to say that our family's theme song was, "We Can't Afford It, We Can't Afford It, We Can't Afford It." No matter what came up, we couldn't afford it, so my parents bought used clothes from Goodwill and St. Vincent de Paul because they couldn't afford new clothes. I didn't have any new clothes for 10 years. They'd get us used clothes even for birthdays and Christmas.

Now the worst experience I ever had was when I was wearing some of my throw-away clothes to school and some other kids recognized that their parents had given those clothes to Goodwill, and here's Tracy wearing the clothes that they gave to the Goodwill. Everybody laughed. I still remember that. Ha, ha, ha, ha everybody laughed. And as I walked around that day, people pointed at me, "There's the guy that wears the Goodwill clothes." I was 11 or 12 at that time, and I still remember.

Your belief system is really, really important. What you believe and what you expect of yourself determines virtually everything you do. The messages that you receive as a young person are just accepted by the subconscious mind as fact, and then they become your operating principles. So I was told over and over again, if you don't get good grades, you won't be successful in life. If you don't get good grades, you won't go to college. If you don't go to college, you won't get a good job. If you don't go to college and earn good money, you won't marry well. You'll just be looking at laboring jobs.

So I began to look around the neighborhood, and I saw a lot of other kids who had much better lives, their homes looked better, they drove newer cars, they had better clothes and they had more money.

Scene: Brian speaking to audience

One of the things that I've found is that everybody has turning points in life. I was living in a small, one-room apartment where you had to fold down the bed, and it had a little kitchen, and it was 35 degrees outside. I was working carrying materials on a construction job, and I'd get up at five o'clock in the morning and start taking buses. It

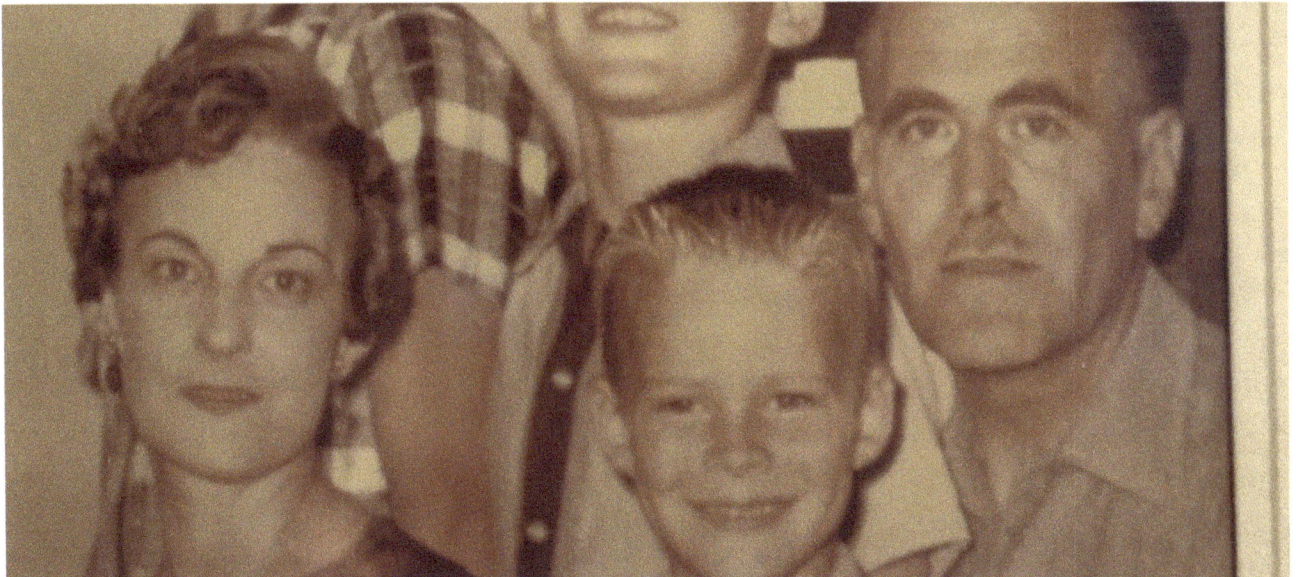

took me three buses to get to my workplace, and then it would take me three buses to get back, so I'd get back by about seven or eight in the evening. By this time, I didn't have any money, and I would be tired from all the heavy lifting. That's all I was educated enough to do is carry building materials.

One day, I sat at my little table in my little kitchen, and I'm tired, and that's when I had this revelation: I realized that this was my life. That unless I changed or did something different, this was going to be my life. I looked at the people who worked on the construction crew—some of them were 30 or 40-years-old, and they were still doing the same basic, minimum-wage construction work and I realized that I was responsible for my own life. Even to this day, I still remember that, almost like fireworks: I am responsible. I am responsible. I am responsible. Nothing will change unless I change.

The next day, I bought five textbooks. I bought a book on abnormal psychology. I bought a book on history. I bought a book on physics. I just bought books. I took them home and I got a pen, and I began to read them and study them every night. When other people would go out socializing and everything else in the evening, I'd come home from my work and I would study for two to three hours. I'd sit at my desk and I'd work. And I loved to do it. I loved to learn new things.

After I'd been doing this for a month, I was working on the construction job, and the big boss came along. He was big and rich, and he was beautifully dressed. It was cold outside, and he had on this beautiful coat. He was a very nice guy and he stopped and he said to me, "How are you? What's your name?" I said, "Brian."

I knew who he was. Everybody knew he was the big boss. He said, "How long have you been working here?" He asked me a couple of questions, and then he said, "Well, nice talking to you," and he went away. Then he turned around and he came back and said, "Brian, you shouldn't be working here. You've got to get out of here and do something better. You've got so much more potential than just carrying building materials," and he turned and walked away. That was one of the most important moments of my life. It was very close to the same time I realized that I was responsible.

"IT CHANGED MY LIFE FOREVER."

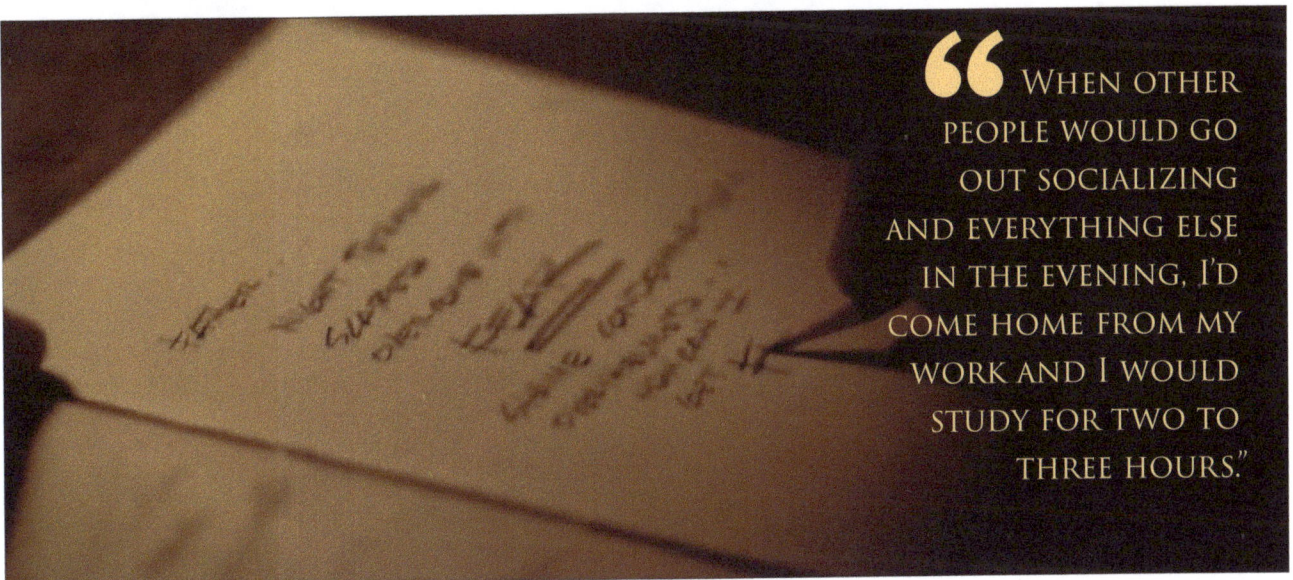

> **"** When other people would go out socializing and everything else in the evening, I'd come home from my work and I would study for two to three hours."

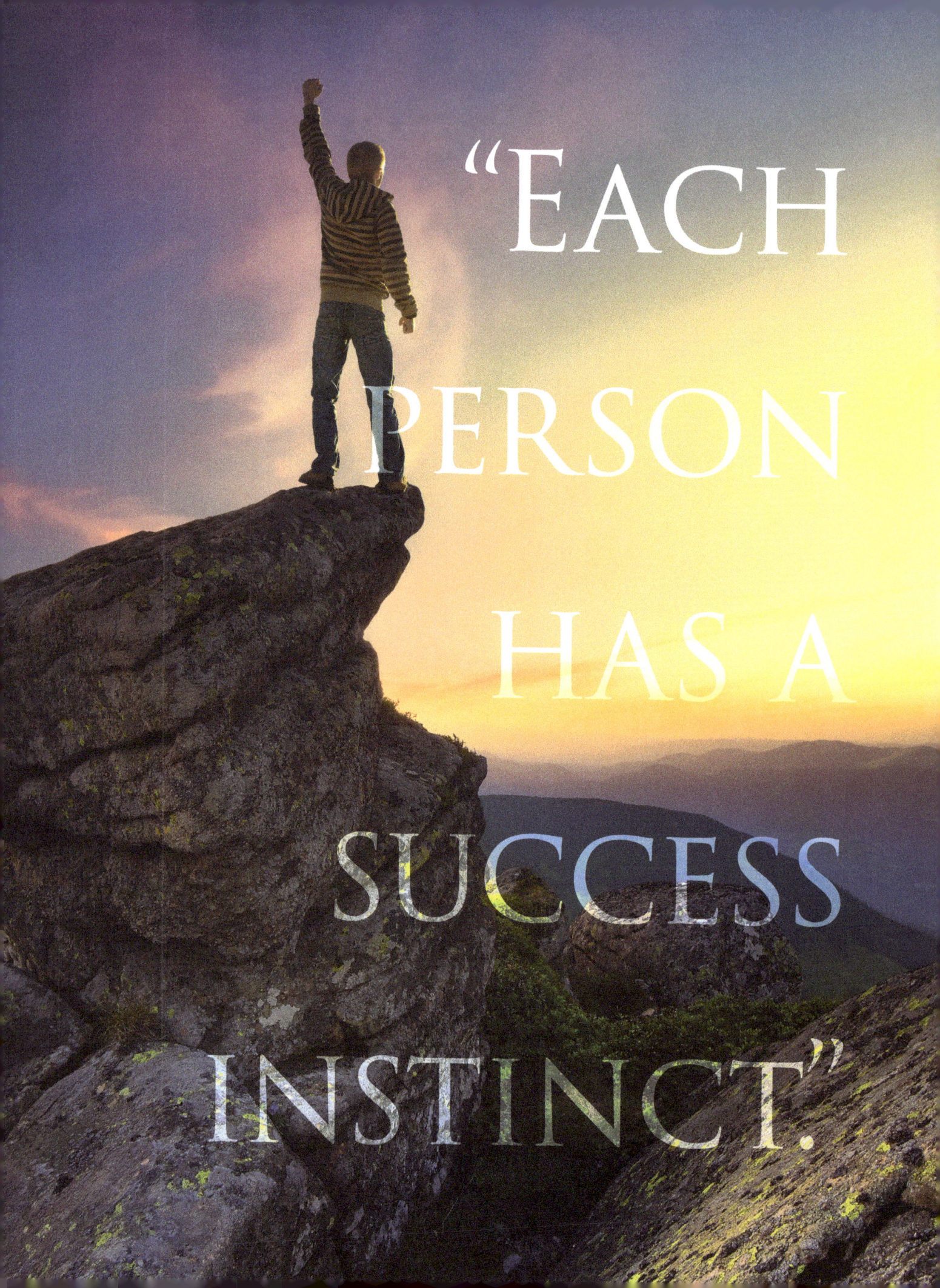

"EACH PERSON HAS A SUCCESS INSTINCT."

" Human beings are designed by nature to succeed. We say that they are designed by nature to survive, so the most pressing desire a human being has is to survive.

Abraham Maslow transformed the understanding of human motivation with his pyramid. He said the first thing we do is survive, but once we are in a society or safe environment where our life is not at stake, the next thing we go up to is security. We seek security, money, relationships, living accommodations, travel and everything else. Until we can satisfy that need—we have enough money and we're safe enough in our relationships and in our job and so on—until we satisfy that need, we think of nothing else. Most people never get past level two. They're thinking about their security all the time and they have not achieved it. You can have a wonderful life and then you hear that there are lay-offs in your company and a lot of people are going to be laid off, and you immediately go back down to level two of motivation and that's all you think about because you have this instinct to succeed.

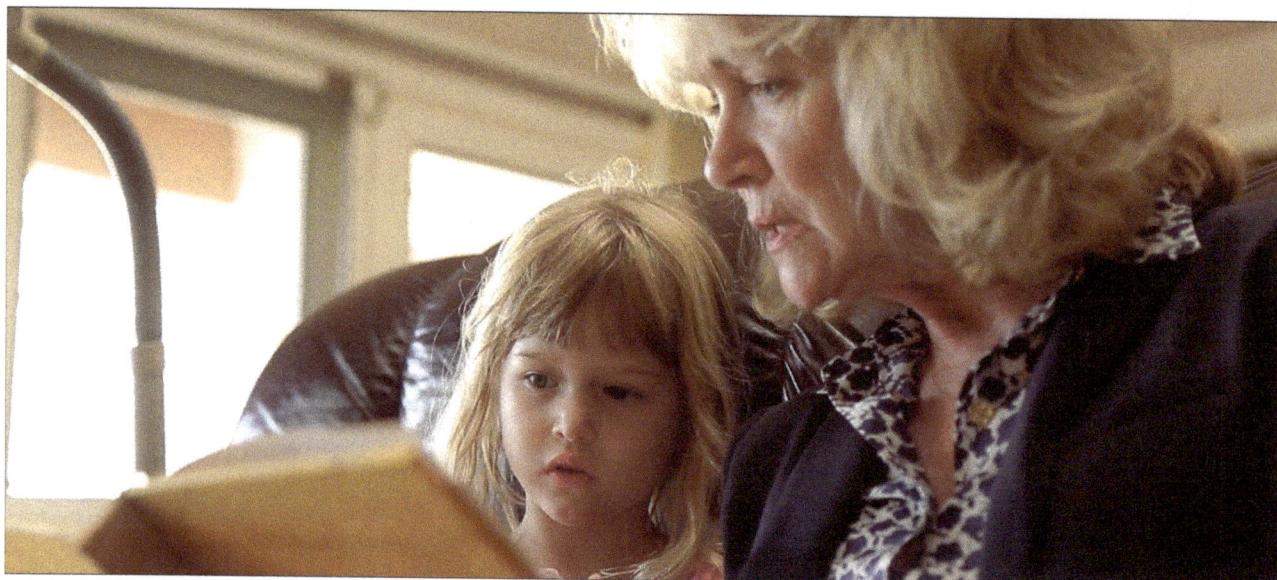

BARBARA TRACY
BRIAN'S WIFE

> **Our definition of failure is not a bad thing. There are no negative connotations to failing. Failing is a way for us to determine what things are not working, so that we can clarify what things can work and do work. One of the things Brian teaches is that you fail your way to success and to be a big success, you have to fail many, many times.**

We've always told our children that we love them unconditionally. We love them all the time, we love them 100%, and there's nothing they could do that would take our love away. Our love would never be conditional. Brian didn't start out with that kind of a background. His background was definitely

conditional. If he was quiet and was almost unseen, they approved. If he wasn't and he was a normal child and did normal things and got into trouble, they did not approve. So he spent a lot of time feeling not good enough. He came to the conclusion as an adult, and through his reading, that you can change this.

Scene Footage of past speaking event

BRIAN TRACY

Barbara and I came across this article a few years ago—it was an interview with an analyzing psychiatrist who had worked with unhappy people for 25 years. He was a very prominent social psychiatrist, who worked with top people, and he said the most common words he ever heard when someone came to him for counseling were the words, "if only." If only my father, if only my mother, if only I had, if only I hadn't, if only they, if only this, if only that. He said the words "if only" preceded an entire lifetime of grief. So what we did is we made a decision—no more "if onlys." No more "if onlys" in life. Never say that phrase again. As far as we're concerned, let the past bury the past. The past is gone. No more "if onlys" in your life.

Scene Brian speaking to audience

One of the best expressions to eliminate fear of any kind are those words "I can do it. I can do it. I can do it. I can do it."

I was reading a throw away book, and it said if you want to be successful, you've got to have goals. So I found a scrap of paper and I wrote down the date and ten goals that

> "One of the best expressions to eliminate fear of any kind are the words "I can do it.""

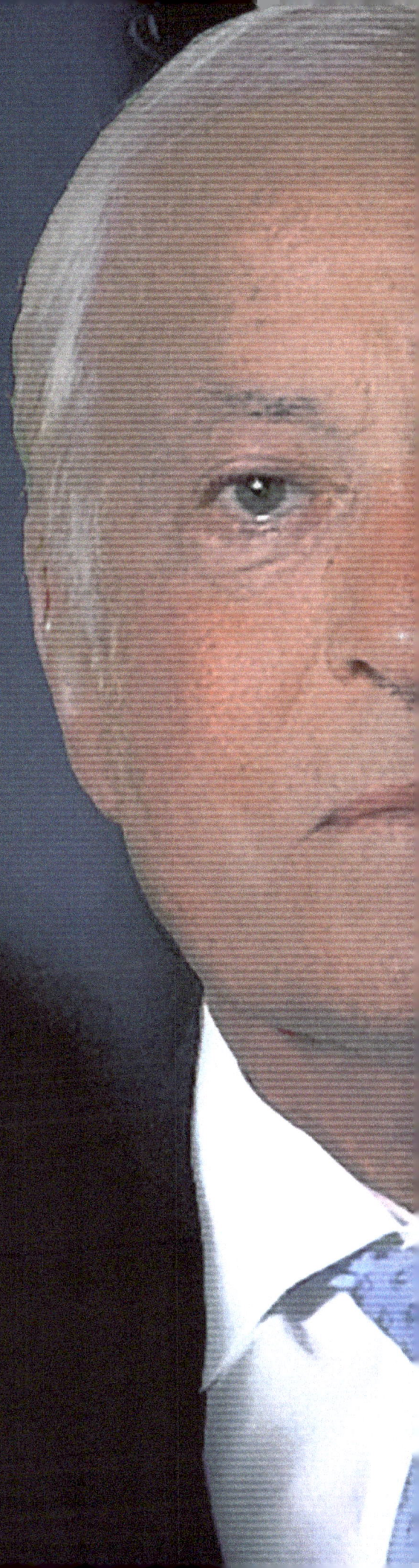

I would like to achieve. And I promptly lost the piece of paper. But within 30 days, I had gotten a job in selling. And then I got another job in selling. I found a technique of closing sales that was marvelous. Within a month, I was earning $1,000 a month. I was put in charge of 32 sales people. I was running a sales team, and I was 24-years-old. Within another month, I had my own apartment. I had new clothes. I had money in my pocket. I was going to night clubs and restaurants.

It was miraculous what happened with goals, and what they do is they give you this incredible feeling of, "I can do anything I put my mind to." It was like an explosion again. I couldn't believe that goals are so powerful. However, you have to write it down for it to work, you can't type it out. As a matter of fact, more and more university professors are banning the use of laptops in class because if all you do is type what the professor says, it bypasses your conscious mind. You don't remember any of it. You're just retyping the words. If you have to write them down, you have to think about the sentence structure and the key points and the way it's phrased. Then when you go back and read it, it triggers your memory.

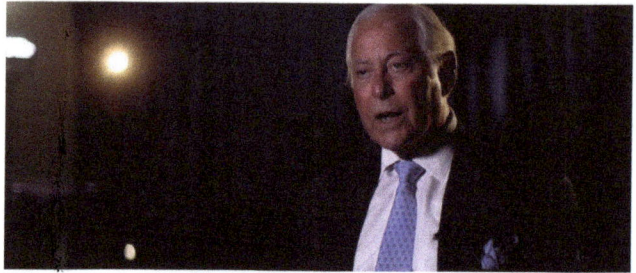

"I CAN DO ANYTHING I PUT MY MIND TO."

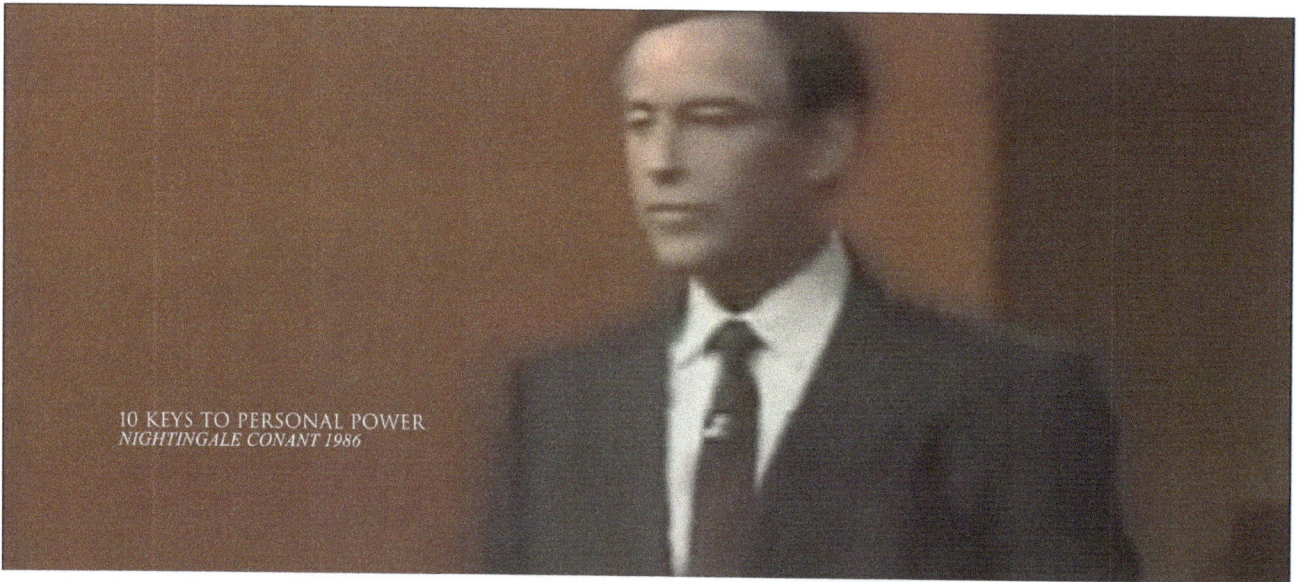

10 KEYS TO PERSONAL POWER
NIGHTINGALE CONANT 1986

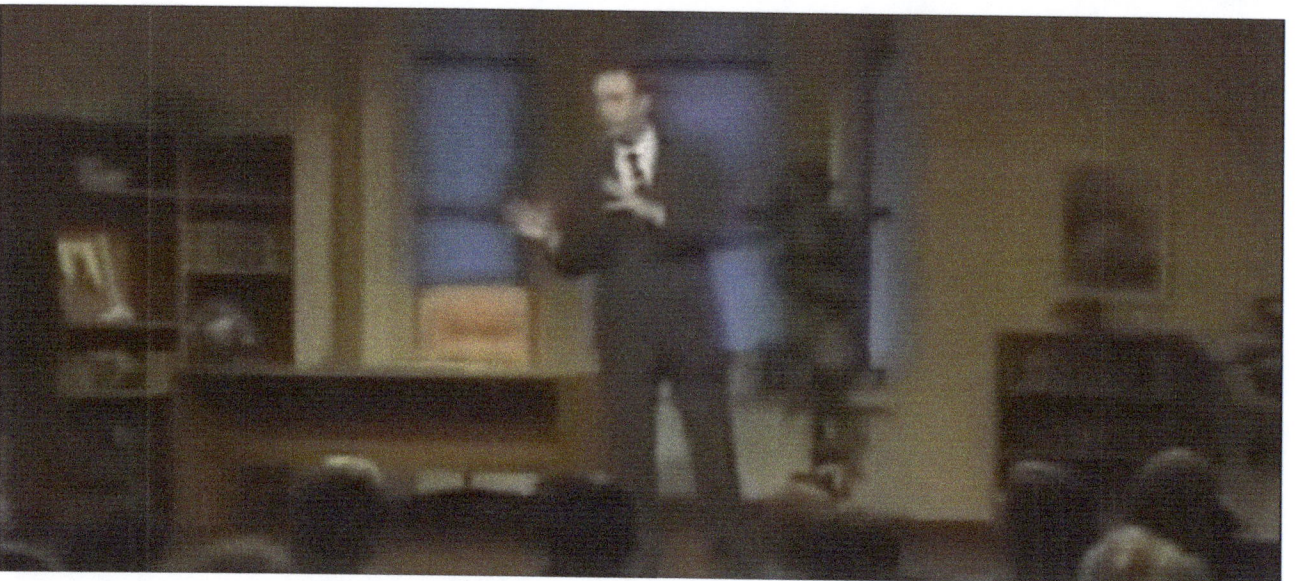

"A WISH IS MERELY A GOAL WITHOUT ANY ENERGY BEHIND IT"

Scene: Brian speaking at Nightingale Conant

BRIAN TRACY All goals have to be in writing, by the way. If you don't have your goals in writing, then they're not really goals at all. They're merely wishes, and as they say, a wish is merely a goal without any energy behind it. Have your goals in writing. Write them out very specifically and clearly, and then do this: every single morning, rewrite your major goals in the first-person singular as though they already exist. Rewrite your major goals every single morning. Now, this should take you two to four minutes, maybe five. You can do it all in a paragraph. For instance, if your goal is to earn $50,000 a year, then every single morning write, "I earn $50,000 a year." If your goal is to be excellent in real estate say, "I am an excellent salesperson in my field." If your goal is to weigh a certain number of pounds, if your goal is to enjoy a certain kind of life, write down your major goals in the first-person singular as though they already exist today, every single morning.

Then every single evening, take about five or ten minutes, instead of watching television or just before you turn on the television say, "Wait a second. I've got to review my progress." Sit down and review what you've done in the course of the day and say, "What have I done right today? What have I done right that's moved me toward my goals?" Second question is, "What would I do differently if I had today to do over again?" If you'll ask yourself those two questions, in the next 30 days you'll accomplish more than you accomplished in the last six months.

Each time you take an action toward a goal your self-confidence goes up. You feel more positive. You think, "Hey, I can do this. I can do this." The old saying is, "It ain't bragging if you've done it." When you actually start to make progress towards your goal, your self-confidence and self-esteem go up. Once you have this belief that I can do this, no matter what happens I can do this, then nothing can stop you. Failure is not an option.

"

The thing I love about Brian—the thing that he really hammers home, whether he says it directly or through all his messages: is nothing can be accomplished without putting in the work. There's so many things, like the fitness industry that wants to talk about how you can get six pack abs overnight. Well, we all know that's not going to happen. There's not anything you can do to do it, you've just got to put in the work and have the discipline."

WEST SEEGMILLER, ESQ.
TRIAL ATTORNEY
SAN DIEGO, CA

"

One thing he said is there's not one thing. Being successful in your personal life, in your relationships, in your business is a series of things that you have to do over time. When people ask him is there one thing that you can tell me today that I can do, he says, 'Yeah, one thing I can tell you is there's not one thing.'"

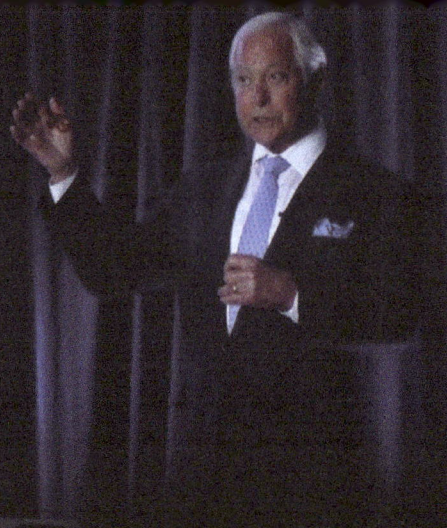

1. Peace of Mind

You can imagine that life is like a recipe and that recipe has seven ingredients. If you make the dish without one of the key ingredients, the flavor will be gone. Very much like when you make bread, it has many ingredients, but it also has yeast and if the yeast is missing then the bread is just flat.

Many people have many of the ingredients necessary for great success, but they're just missing one or two skills; one or two pieces of knowledge, which are very easy to obtain.

There are seven ingredients of success, and I've studied this from thousands of books and articles and I've found there are seven things that embrace everything that people seek.

WHY AREN'T YOU AT PEACE?

What would you have to do differently to enjoy a greater level of peace?

The first is peace of mind. Now, this is the foundational principle of all religions, all philosophies, all discussions of personal relationships and all works on personal growth and development: for a person to achieve peace of mind. To be at peace is to be happy, to be just calm. You'll find that as human beings we strive continually to create a world around ourselves that enables us to feel at peace. In fact, you can actually give yourself a grade of how well you're doing at life by how often or what percentage of the time you feel really happy and at peace with your life.

Then of course, if you're not at peace, why not? Why aren't you at peace? What would you have to do differently to enjoy a greater level of peace? I spent 4,000 hours, almost my whole 20s, studying this area of psychology. The only thing between you and complete happiness and success and everything else is negative emotions. That's the major barrier that blocks you from getting there.

Then I learned two things. First, no one is born with any negative emotions and second, all negative emotions are un-learnable. They've all been learned, so you can unlearn them. You can cancel them. You can just basically pluck them out of your life forever and in the absence of negative emotions, your life fills with positive emotions because nature abhors a vacuum, even an emotional vacuum.

You're like, "Wow, this sounds like pretty simple stuff." Yes. I used to say that God only made simple people, so all these principles are simple. They're not complicated principles. Whether we use them or not is a different thing.

Scene: Brian speaking to camera

When my father died, it was very traumatic because I got the news over the telephone. I had made peace with my father, so even though he was not a good father, he was a good man. He'd just been brought up in a terrible situation and he was the result. He never

47

questioned his way of treating children, even though he knew nothing about raising children. I doubt if he ever read one paragraph on how to raise happy kids, but I gave it up.

I remember I was going out with a girl, when I was single. That's very important. I started to complain about my father. This was three or four years before he had died. I started to complain and she said, "Are you happy with your life?" And I said, "Yes, I am." She said, "Well, your father got you here, so shut up." And I never complained about my father again, the rest of my life. If I'm happy with my life, why should I complain about the person who got me here?

▐ Scene: Brian Tracy interview

In 2010 I broke all my best advice. I got into a very bad business deal where I lost a large amount of money. I had placed a lot of hope on this money, sort of like putting all your money on the card table. I placed all my money on this card coming up and the person I was working with was a complete incompetent.

He would not listen to anybody and he did completely stupid things and burned up all the money and bankrupted the company. I was just left there so angry because I'd said, "You can't do this, you can't do this. I teach business, this is not going to work."

And he would always dismiss me. He'd always say, "You don't know what you're talking about. You don't understand this business. You don't understand what you're talking about," and then he would just proceed anyway.

Well, nine months later, I was diagnosed with cancer. I've read 21 textbooks on cancer by the way, and exactly as the textbooks said, six to 21 months after a traumatic event, the first signs of cancer appeared. The first signs of cancer will usually appear based on what kind of traumatic event it was.

2. HEALTH & ENERGY

Health and energy is the second most important thing. The major cause of negative health in most cases in life, about 85% according to the doctors, is negative emotions.

As my friend Dennis Whitley used to say, your medical problems are not caused by what you're eating, but by what's eating you. The gerontologists today are talking about people who reach older age and pointing out that 70-80% of your medical problems are caused by the things that you are doing more or less of or starting or not stopping.

In order to change your health, what you do is you have to change the health habits that are causing the health.

BARBARA When Brian was first diagnosed with throat cancer, we were in a bit of a state of shock for the first 48 hours or so because you just don't expect it. It was throat cancer and he's a professional speaker...this is what he does, this is what he loves to do. There was a lot of silence getting through that first 48 hours. But because of what he teaches and what he knows about changing your destiny, he decided to recover and beat cancer.

BRIAN I got cancer in my throat, and so I went to an Ayurvedic doctor and I said, "I've got throat cancer." She said, "Oh, right side or left side?" I said, "Right side." She said, "Right side in men is caused by money problems, cancer on the left side is caused by relationship problems because the left brain affects the money and the right brain affects the emotions."

So, women mostly have cancer on the left side, men mostly have cancer on the right side. And she says, "You probably had a financial reversal sometime in the last few months." This is a nice little old Indian lady who then said, "Next, please."

By the way, I knew she was correct.

MICHAEL TRACY
BRIAN'S SON

"

When he got throat cancer, it was a real wake up call. We always knew he was tough, but growing up there's this concept that your father or your mother, your parents are invincible—that nothing can ever happen to them. So when he got throat cancer and he started going through treatments, you saw him physically change.

The chemo and radiation...he lost his hair, he got pale, he got weak. That was a real emotional time for the entire family and I think it brought us all closer together. At the same time, he still charged forward. He was still going out and doing talks."

CHRISTINA STEIN
BRIAN'S DAUGHTER

" My dad was like a terminator. He's very committed as a speaker. One of his speaking engagements was during a time where he was supposed to get chemotherapy and he was very adamant that he would not miss this speaking engagement. They gave him this little thing that went around his waist and it was like a chemotherapy box and it would inject a dosage of chemotherapy over a period of a couple days and he wore this to Europe and did a seminar and performed and was great. Nobody knew anything about it."

> **WHAT I FOUND IS THIS, LIFE IS
> ALWAYS JUST IN THE LONG RUN.**
> Therefore, life says there's a price you
> have to pay and there are two qualities.
> First of all, you have to pay the price,
> in full, for your success—comprised
> of study, preparation, hard work and
> so on. Second of all, you have to pay
> the price in advance. You don't get it
> afterwards. The way the world works is
> first you put in what you need to put in
> and then you get out the rewards. So
> you have to ask yourself, what is the
> price that you have to pay to achieve
> the success that you desire?"

MICHAEL He's always said discipline is like a muscle. It's something that you exercise and it gets stronger, and I think maybe it's potentially because he's exercised it over a lifetime, and so he's got an incredibly strong will.

I hope to be able to get to that point, but I don't know anybody who's more hard working or more disciplined than he is.

BARBARA You recognize that emotions can create this and they can get rid of it. So he decided to accept responsibility and decided that he'd forgive this person and move past it.

BRIAN I just let it all go. I just let it go. I even forgot the person's name. I just let it all go, and I went to a doctor and I took all the tests and the biopsies.

He says, "Yeah, you have cancer, and here's the treatment schedule. You follow the treatment schedule. You'll be speaking again as a speaker within six months."

BARBARA Radiation, chemotherapy, he did everything. Toward the end of the radiation, when they did the examination to see how his throat was, it was gone. Completely gone.

BRIAN The sixth month, the 180th day, I was speaking to 800 people in Singapore. I have never had another problem.

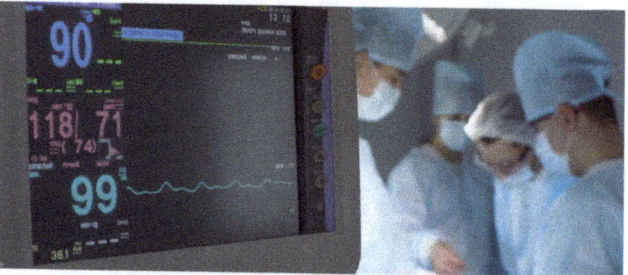

"EVERYTHING THAT

BRIAN

Everything that happens is part of a great process. It's like W. Clement Stone used to say that whenever anything went wrong, that's good. It's all part of a process, so when you absolutely believe that you're going to be a success no matter what happens to you, you'll see it as part of the process, no matter how many setbacks you'll have, you'll see it as part of the process of being successful.

Now if you have influence over other people, the most wonderful thing you could do is tell them that you believe that they're going to be successful.

I have four wonderful children and I learned this before I had my first child, so I've been practicing it on my kids. Because kids are completely amenable to input when they're young, so from the time they were little, I've told them, when you grow up, you're gonna be a big success. When you grow up, you're gonna be a big success.

As they got a little bit older, they said, "Well how am I gonna be a success, Daddy? I don't know what I'm gonna do." "Don't worry, whatever you do, you'll be a big success," I said. "Well what if it doesn't work out?" And I said, "If it doesn't work out, that means something else is where you'll be a big success."

So that's all my kids ever hear. You're going to be a big success. Now, my son David was a little bit shy when he was growing up. I used to tell him, "You're gonna be a big success." And I remember him talking to a friend of his when he was 12, and his friend says, "What are you gonna you do when you grow up, David?"

He said, "Well I don't know, but I'm gonna be a big success." And I said, "It worked! Damn. It worked!"

3. LOVING RELATIONSHIPS

Barbara and I met Ken Blanchard in a restaurant recently, and we were each with our families, and he came over. We talked, and because we've been friends for many years, I said to him, "What have you found is the most important thing in life?" Because Barbara and I were just talking about the most important thing in life.

Barbara and I had concluded it was loving relationships. It was having people that we loved, and having a wonderful family with married kids that love each other. And Ken said, before knowing about our conversation, "Loving relationships are the most important thing in life."

BRIAN I started to take this MBA program at the University of Alberta, and I had written down a description of the perfect woman for me. Actually, I'd done this about five or six years ago, and I had left something off this list. I found the perfect woman based on my description, but the one thing I left off was pleasant temperament. And this woman was an absolute witch. She was just a witch. She was wild, she was literally out of control, I mean shouting, screaming, erratic, everything else.

The next time I wrote the list I said, "Pleasant, very pleasant, very very pleasant. Normal, nice, lovely personality. Good qualities, warm, friendly, cheerful, stable." I mean, I wrote it all down.

BARBARA Brian was taking an MBA degree, and I was studying abnormal psychology. When he came into the room, everybody noticed. He had a very strong sense of his self-concept. In that sense, you know, you couldn't not notice it.

BRIAN Later, I saw her again, we would have coffee together, and I was just a friendly person. She said, "Well, you know, how do you find the perfect person in life?" I said, "What you do is take a sheet of paper and you write it down, you make a list out of everything that you want in the perfect person."

That was just a throwaway piece of advice that I practiced myself. About two or three months later, she called me up and we sat down and she said, "Well, I did what you told me to do. Write down the perfect person for me."

I said, "Well, that's great. That's wonderful." I said, "What did you come with?" She said, "It's you."

BARBARA He was charming. What can I say?

BRIAN I said, "Really? It's me?" we've been married for over 39 years now. Later on we compared lists, and everything I wrote on my list Barbara has and everything Barbara wrote on her list, I had.

Scene: Brian Speaking To Audience

You know who buys all the books on love? 98% are bought by women because men think, "Oh, I know how. Eh, it's just as natural as riding a bicycle. I don't need any instruction." You know why men read books? It's because women give it to them. They give them the book. They buy them for presents. They send it to them. Read this book.

Every man's got a pile of books on relationships that they're meaning to get to.

EDWARD FITZGERALD
ENTREPRENEURIAL TECHNOLOGIST
SOUTHAMPTON, UK

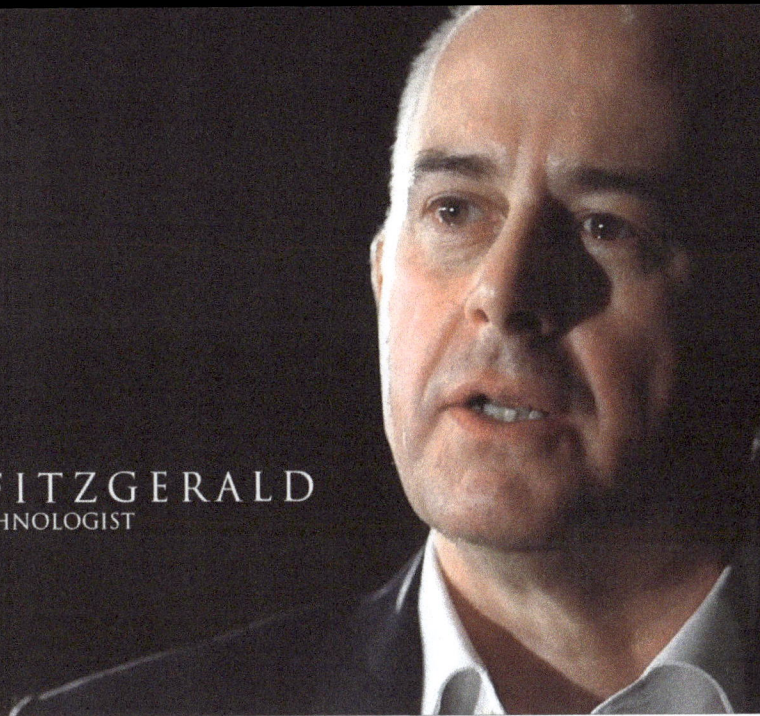

"It was quite late actually. It was probably about 2008 that I started to get into personal development and Brian Tracy along with Jim Rohn and Zig Ziglar were the classic reading for me. In fact, I turned my car into a mobile university. I have all the audiobooks and stuff. It sticks. My kids complain. "Can we have the radio on now, Dad? Who's this old guy talking?" It is going in subconsciously to them as well."

4. FINANCIAL FREEDOM

Number four is financial freedom. One of our goals in life is to achieve financial freedom, and I began to study millionaires and billionaires for years and years and years. I have programs and books and courses on their habits, but one of the things I found about self-made millionaires, is they spend a lot of time thinking about how to become financially independent, whereas most people spend most of the time thinking about how to spend their money.

The average person spends about an hour a month thinking about their money, usually at the end of the month when they're paying their bills, and they bitch and complain and whine about how much everything costs, and who spent this, and who bought that.

Then they think about how much they're going to pay off on their credit card each month, and they pay a little bit down here and there. Rich people spend 10 hours per month just studying the magazines, the financial programs, which have some of the smartest financial people. They read the *Wall Street Journal* and *Business Week* and they make notes and then they read books on how to earn more money and how to accumulate it and how to invest it.

So a person who's spending 10 times as much as an average person learning and studying has got an edge. They've got an edge that the average person can never catch up with, and at a certain point in their 20s and 30s, their financial resources begin to grow. By their 40s and their 50s, people who start in their 20s, are financially independent, and now they're working for fun and they're working for love. They're doing things they enjoy, which surprisingly enough, pays a lot more than anything else.

Scene: Speaking at Self Made Millionaires 2005

BRIAN

One of the things that I learned, by the way, is that becoming a self-made millionaire is not the important thing. What is really important is the person you have to become to become a self-made millionaire. You have to become a totally different human being.

One of my friends says that in order to achieve something you've never achieved before, you have to become someone you've never been before. And it's a really important insight, the qualities you need to develop to become a self-made millionaire are incredible qualities on the inside that make you a vastly better person.

Scene: Speaking at Nightingale Conant 1987

BRIAN

Now no matter what field you're in, no matter what field of endeavor, no matter what work, no matter what activity, there's one thing that all successful people have in common and it's that they are good time managers. And the reason they are good time managers is because they recognize that

"TIME MANAGEMENT IS LIFE MANAGEMENT AND IT IS PERSONAL MANAGEMENT."

Scene: Speaking to audience

BRIAN (Speaking to audience)

What we've found is people in the top 10% in every field think in terms of their hourly rate, how much I earn each hour. Now this change in thinking changes your entire life. I know it because I've taught this principle to thousands of people who literally transformed their lives and their incomes almost overnight.

If you think in terms of how much you earn in a week or a month, well then you have a natural tendency to waste time during the day. Monday is a slow day, you're recovering from the weekend. Tuesday you start to work, Wednesday the week is almost over, Thursday you start to slow down, and now it's Friday, who gets anything done on Friday? We'll do it Monday. So people's ability to produce drops, drops, and drops. And since 80% of the population thinks like this, if you're not careful, you'll find you are surrounded by people who waste time. The biggest time wasters in the world are other people who want to waste your time.

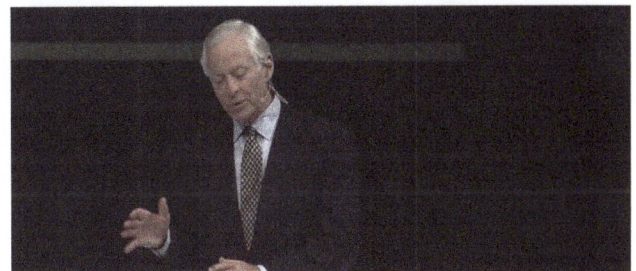

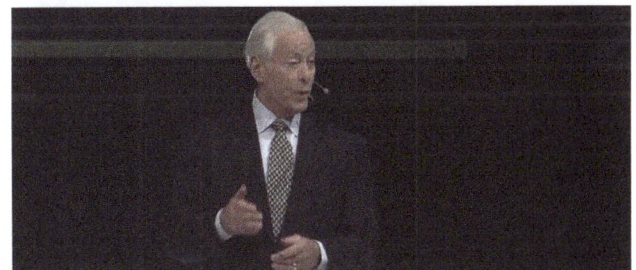

Scene: Speaking to audience

BRIAN

I say this, your television can make you rich or it can make you poor. It can make you rich if you turn it off. Watch it occasionally, use it as a tool, catch up with the news, maybe watch an hour of entertainment. Rich people watch about one hour of television per day. Poor people watch five to seven hours, and so rich people basically watch an hour to decompress in the evening and then go to bed. Poor people watch television until they can't watch without falling asleep.

"YOUR TELEVISION CAN MAKE YOU RICH OR IT CAN MAKE YOU POOR."

Scene: Speaking to audience

BRIAN

I don't know about you, but I see *Oprah's* on in the afternoon. If you're watching *Oprah*, it means your life sucks! You don't have a life, so all the people watching *Oprah* are people who are at home in the afternoon, who have nothing going on. God bless her. Oprah could come and go and Oprah could be on the front pages of every newspaper for 50 years and have zero effect on your life. I just think, "What's the matter with them?" You could be spending time with the people you care about. If you spend as much time with your kids as many people spend with Oprah you'd have a wonderful family.

🎬 **Scene:** Speaking to audience

Rich people get up before 6:00 in the morning. They hit the ground running at 6:00 AM. Poor people get up with an hour to get to work and scramble and racing, beep, beep, beep, and so on.

You just start to look at the research that they're doing. It's just the way they think. Cause and effect says that if you get up early, exercise, plan your day, and get started, you'll accomplish two or three or five times as much as people who race to work at the last minute, coming in and spending 50% of that time talking to their friends, checking their email all day long, and then go home early to beat the traffic—they are the traffic.

🎬 **Scene:** Speaking to interviewer

BRIAN

The law of correspondence says that your outer world will be a reflection of your inner world, and this is a law. It's 1 to 1. It's my favorite ratio. As the Bible says, "As within so without." "As he thinketh in his heart, so is he." In other words, it's what's going on inside of you that determines what happens on the outside.

If you want to earn more money on the outside, become more valuable on the inside. Serve more people and serve them at a higher level.

MUTHU MUDALIAR
RETIREMENT SOLUTIONS EXPERT
FRISCO, TX

"

I am in the financial services business. My motto always was, independent of Brian, spread knowledge and also help create wealth for millions of people. Because of my God-given talent I am more fortunate than billions of people, so with my remaining life I want to spread the message."

TAMARA MAGALOTTI
FINANCIAL & BUSINESS CONSULTANT
SAN FRANCISCO, CA

"

The one thing that I think stuck out the most is that it is a process. It doesn't happen overnight. You need to create a plan and actually work on that plan. You can't just have wishful thinking and write down your goals and think, 'My goals are going to come.' It doesn't happen that way. You have to have a plan and take action."

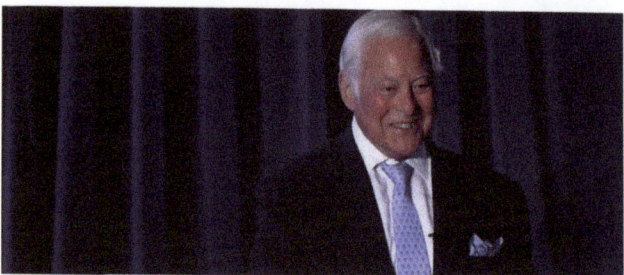

BRIAN

Financial freedom means that you don't worry about money because you have enough money so that you don't ever have to worry about money again. I used to start off a business seminar and say, "What would it mean to you if you had enough money so that you never would have to worry about it again for the rest of your life?" I'd just throw out the question and leave it. This question hits people like an emotional wave. Everybody goes dead silent because they think, "Oh my God, if had that much money, I would be doing things totally different than what I'm doing in my life today. I'd be doing more of this and less of that. I'd start doing this and I'd stop doing that."

"

Me and my friends used to go into the pond by the golf course and collect golf balls and then clean them off and go to the first hole and sell them back to the golfers. I think one of the golfers called and complained that we were there setting up shop trying to sell golf balls and my dad's like, 'What were you doing?'

I told him and he's like, 'You're not providing enough value. You need to have cold waters with golf balls. You're trying to sell these golf balls for a dollar a ball. It's expensive. You need to offer them something with it.' He just changed our business model; we didn't really stop doing it, but little things like that he would just come up with and it was great. Every little problem that I'd have, he'd approach it with all this experience and I'd be able to see it in a different way."

73

Scene: Speaking to audience

BRIAN

I was never good at anything. I was never picked for any team. If I was picked, I was the first person cut. I got lousy grades in every class. I got fired from multiple jobs. I even got fired from a job pumping gas. Imagine that, being fired for pumping gas because you're no good. They came out and said

Scene: Speaking to audience

BRIAN

Later, I got into real estate development and I knew nothing about real estate development and didn't even have any money.

I went down to the library, that was the time when you'd get everything at the library, and I checked out 21 books on real estate

you're no good at pumping gas. How can you be no good? Little old ladies can pump gas, and here I was I was no good at pumping gas. Anyway, I got fired. I went from job to job and then I discovered that all people who are successful are excellent at what they do. You know the old question they asked Willie Sutton, the bank robber, "Why do you rob banks?" He said, "Well, that's where the money is." Well, being in the top 10% is where the money is.

and real estate development over the course of about three months. These were written by the most successful real estate entrepreneurs alive. I took notes and notes and notes and notes and notes and piles and piles of notes on anything that showed how to find a piece of property. Then I went out and I began looking at properties in fast-growing parts of the city, in fast-growing cities and near the big cities and I finally found a perfect piece of property. Then I went out and I began looking at properties in fast-growing areas near the big cities, and I finally found a perfect piece of property. So I went in and interviewed the owner, but first I re-searched… how do you interview an owner who's running a business on the property? And finally they agreed to sell the property to me, and I didn't even have any money. However, I went to the chapter on how do you buy a piece of property when you have no money? Well, what you do is you get the vendor of the property to agree to give you an option to purchase the property at this price with a small down payment. By this time, the couple who owned the property had brought in a lawyer. I still remember the lawyer, he was a great guy. He said,"Brian, they've been in this business long enough. You've got to help them get out." He said, "Just find the money." I said, "I can only find the money if I can have an option on this property for 30 days." He said, "How much can you give me?" I said, "$150." He said, "All right. You give me $150. I'll convince them to give you a 30-day unrestricted op-tion on this property." I said, "You'll do that?" and, "Please don't cash the check." Because I didn't have $150 in the bank. I went out and I want to the next chapter. What do you do when you've tied up a property and you need to find money….And I began calling real estate development companies, rental rates, profitability rates, insurance rates, fi-nancing. I already had the letters of commit-ment that said good we'll put out 100% of the money for 75% of the deal.

That changed my whole life. For the rest of my life, I couldn't believe it. I've devel-oped more than $100 million worth of real estate. People say, "Are you a real estate developer?" No, I just develop the real estate. "Well, how do you do it?" I just read the books, just like stories. Every single suc-cess skill has formulas and they're all learn-able and they're all written down. If a person starts from nothing and stays at nothing, they have only themselves to blame.

Brian meets with people at a special event in San Diego.

BARBARA We attended this personal professional development seminar early in our marriage. It affected our thinking, but Brian felt he could do better. Which is always in the back of his mind, when he sees something he knows he can do it better and I know that he can do better too. We made the decision to create our own two-day personal professional development seminar.

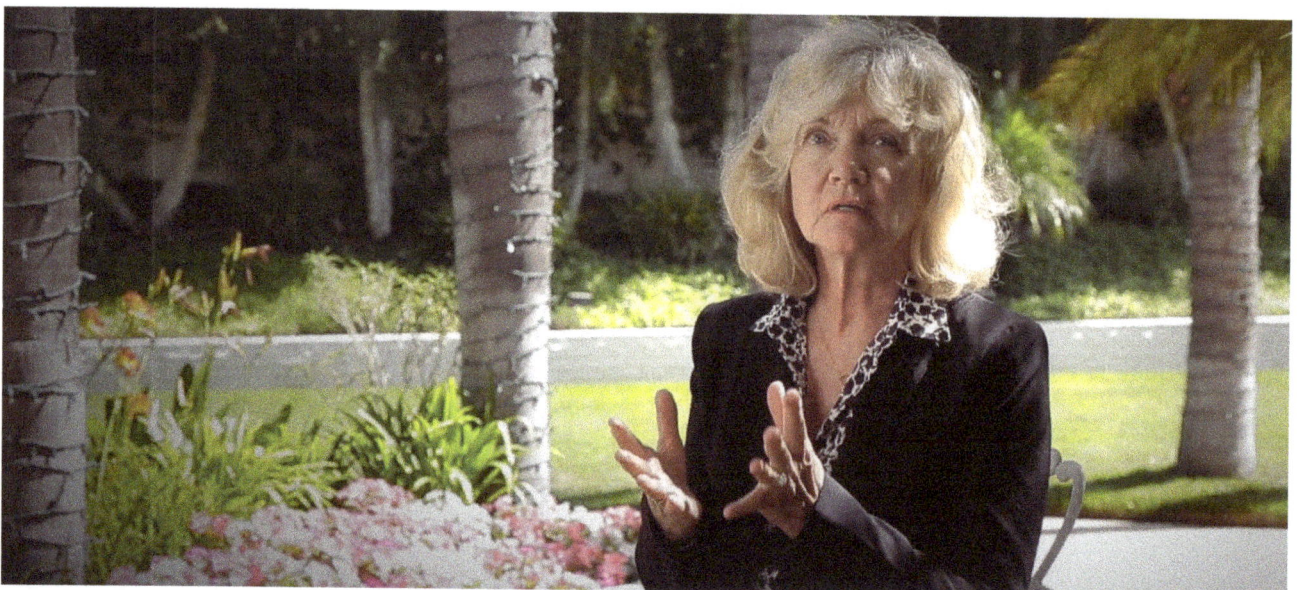

BRIAN

The fact is if you want to be an expert, there's a rule, it's called the law of seven. It's the law of seven years. It takes seven years from the time that you begin to the time that you crack into expert levels. I learned this when I first began speaking. I'd been

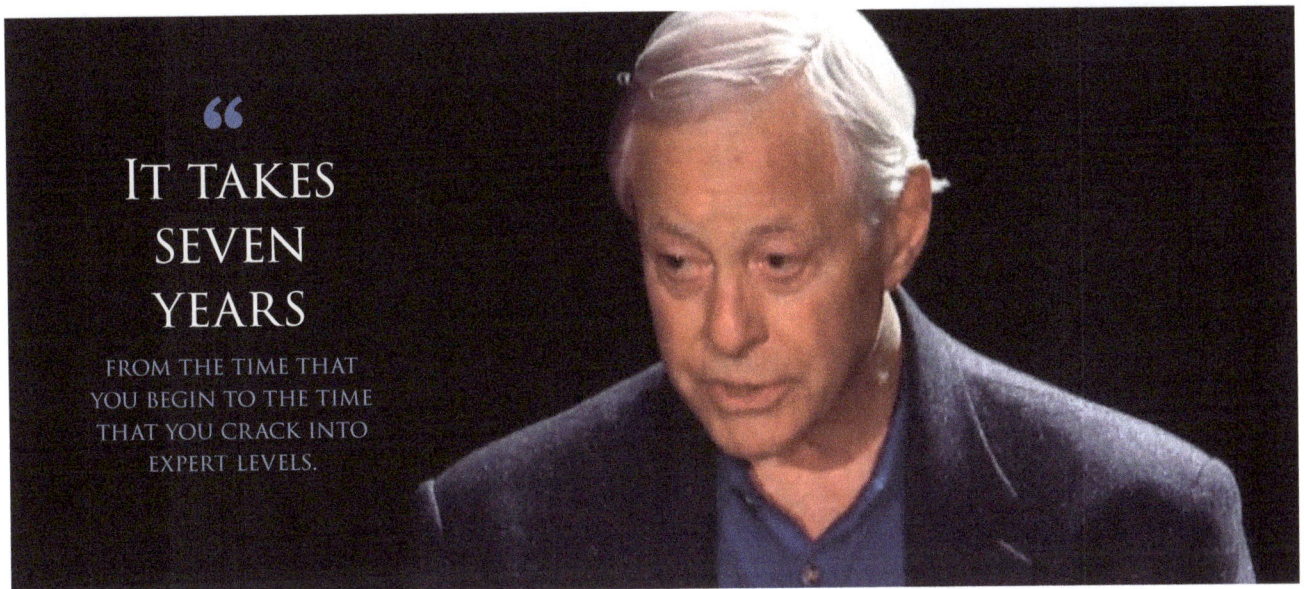

> ## " IT TAKES SEVEN YEARS
>
> FROM THE TIME THAT YOU BEGIN TO THE TIME THAT YOU CRACK INTO EXPERT LEVELS.

speaking for about three years and I was starting to do well. I was now earning more than it was costing me to stay in business. I was no longer paying people to come and listen to me, which I did for the first two years. I used to joke that when I began speaking, I learned how to sell again. I sold my house. I sold my car. I sold my furniture. I sold everything so I could keep feeding my habit. I was like an addict.

BARBARA I remember outside the door, waiting for people to show up and pay money. We used to kid about that particular time and call it sweaty palms time, because you're just waiting for people. How many will come? Will it cover our costs?

Scene: Speaking to interviewer

BRIAN

I was called by a client in my first or second year of speaking and he said, "I have a company with 800 business owners, who are coming to an annual convention and they all want to be rich. Could you do a seminar on self-made millionaires?" At that time, I'd take any talk. I said,"Absolutely. Sure. No problem. I'll do it." I have two months. I hung up the phone and I realized I knew nothing about self-made millionaires. I thought, "Geez, I better start doing some research because this could be a really big client." I was charging them a lot of money. I began to study and I found this enormous amount of research on self-made millionaires, thousands of them have been interviewed and analyzed over the years. Rags to riches, rags to riches. I began to cull out and I began to come up with common threads from all this research. I came up with a program called *The Success Secrets of Self-Made Millionaires."*

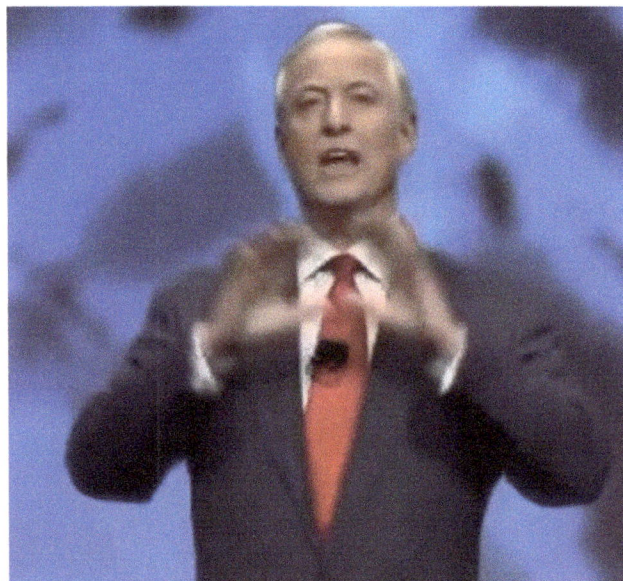

Scene: Speaking at the Self Made Millionaire event.

BRIAN

Give yourself a score of one to 10 and if you are weak on one of these, it can be enough to hold you back. The first is to dream big dreams. Dream big dreams, practice what is called back from the future thinking and project forward, develop a vision of yourself as happy, healthy, wealthy, thin. Practice what top people practice, which is called idealization. You project forward several years and you imagine that your life is perfect in every way. Imagine that you have no limitations. Imagine that you have all the time and all the money and all the friends and all the contacts and all the education and all the experience. Imagine that you could be or have or do anything you want in life.

If you could, what would it be? If your life were perfect in five years, what would it look like? How much would you be earning? How much would you be worth? What kind of a family life would you have? What kind of health would you have? What kind of car would you be driving?

"WHAT WOULD YOUR LIFE BE LIKE IF YOU COULD WAVE A MAGIC WAND AND MAKE IT **PERFECT** IN EVERY WAY?"

KEVIN HODES
CERTIFIED PAYMENT PROFESSIONAL
DALLAS, TX

"
There are so many things that he does, but I'll tell you everything is so common sense. Then when you take those common sense principles and put them into place in your own business and your own life, it'll help you gain the success that you're looking for. But more importantly, I love the fact that he started from humble beginnings and that's the same thing I've started with. And then moving forward, being successful, and sharing it with others."

"When you hear somebody like that talking, he's a wordsmith, he's a teacher, he's an educator. My business has a lot of those same characteristics. A lot of what he says you say, 'Oh, I know that,' but the way that he puts things and the way that he ties everything together is very unique, very unique to his experience. There's nobody in the world, I think, who knows more about wealthy, successful, happy people than Brian Tracy."

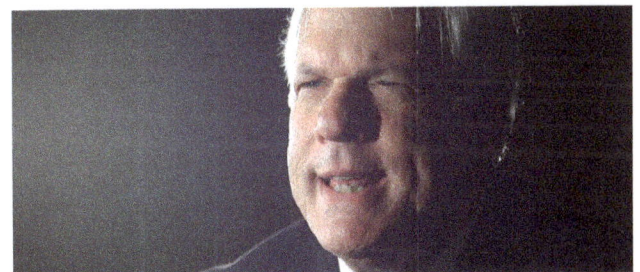

FAI CHAN
CLINICAL AROMATHERAPIST
LAKEWAY, TX

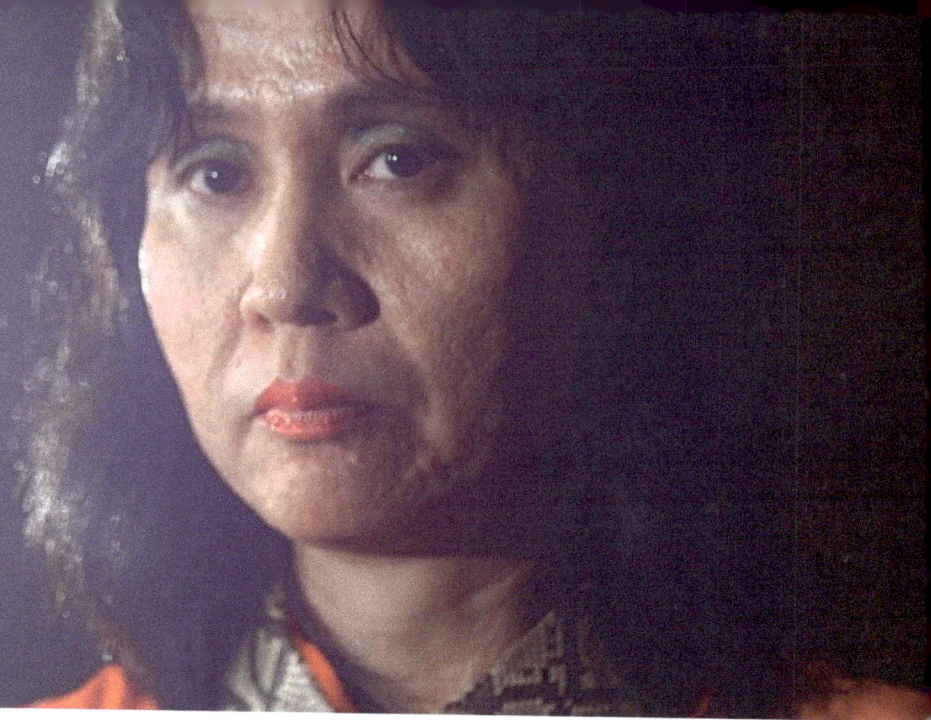

"After my participation I think that I should be more serious about distributing his knowledge to other people so that they can learn from this legendary man in the United States or worldwide."

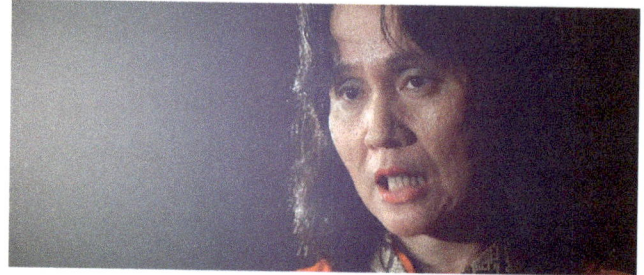

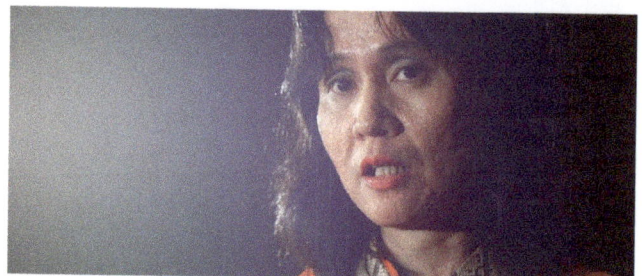

5. WORTHY GOALS & IDEAS

Scene: Speaking to audience

BRIAN

One of my wealthiest friends many years ago said, "Success is goals, and all else is commentary." Success in every part of your life, but of course your financial life, your business life, your home life. Success is goals, and all else is commentary. With regard to goals we say worthy goals and ideals give us a sense of meaning and purpose. Going back to wonderful work that's been done over the years, we know that meaning and purpose is the deepest and most profound subconscious need of the human being—to feel that their lives have a meaning, that they're doing something that means something.

Viktor Frankl was famous for his work after being in both Auschwitz and Birkenau, surviving the concentration camps. That's what he said, "The greatest human need is for meaning and purpose." He said he watched the people in the camps and he said, "As long as they had a meaning, a reason to survive, they survived, but if they gave up hope, they would die very quickly."

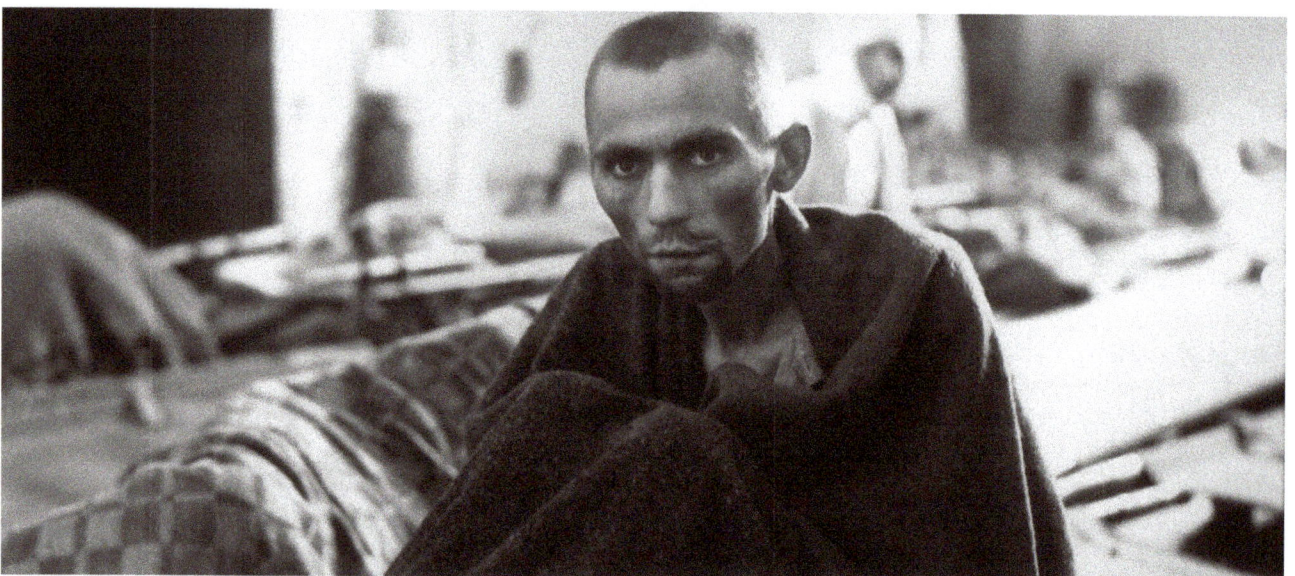

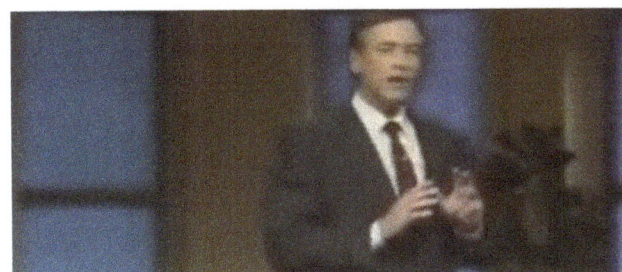

Scene: Speaking to audience

BRIAN

YOU MUST COMMIT YOURSELF TO EXCELLENCE.

You must commit yourself to becoming the best. The wonderful thing is that excellence is a journey. It's not a destination. You never get there. Complacency and satisfaction are the key enemies of excellence, but once you commit yourself to becoming excellent, the whole world opens up for you. By the way, you can tell how excellent you are at any time. Any time of your life you can tell how excellent you are. It's very simple to measure. How many job offers have you had this month? Interesting question. How many job offers? How many people called you and said, "I want to hire you away from where you are and I'll pay you more and give you a better deal?" Because excellent people get job offers every month. Some of them get job offers every single week. If you're not getting job offers, the market is telling you what they think of your level of competence. If you do not love your work enough to want to be the best at it, get out of it the way you would get out of a burning house. Do not stay at a job that you do not love because it is the highroad to failure, dissatisfaction, frustration and unhappiness in life.

ΓΝΩΘΙ ΣΕΑΥΤΟΝ

"KNOW THYSELF"

6. SELF KNOWLEDGE & SELF UNDERSTANDING

Scene: Speaking to audience

BRIAN

The subject must absolutely fascinate you. It must be a subject that you love. It must be a subject that grabs you, because you are unique. As they say, "Be yourself, everyone else is already taken."

Self-knowledge and self-understanding is one of the most important things of all. All of psychology, all of psychotherapy, all of counseling and guidance, coaching, everything else is to help people reach a higher level of personal awareness. In the Delphic Oracle, which was one of the greatest seven wonders of the world, there's a sign. We've been there and it says,

"MAN, KNOW THYSELF." THE MOST IMPORTANT THING IN LIFE IS TO KNOW THYSELF.

The French writer Pascal said, "All the problems of the human race come from not being able to sit alone in a room for an hour." We teach in our seminars the importance of solitude, the importance of going into silence and being completely still for 30 minutes or more and just letting your mind unwind. Don't write, don't smoke, don't listen to music, don't drink coffee, just sit. It's astonishing because as you sit there and as you pass what seems to be the 26th minute of total silence, suddenly ideas start to come to you. Ideas that can change your life, ideas and insights of what to do more or less of or what to start doing and what to stop doing. Really phenomenal stuff.

DAVID We used to do this thing at the dinner table. I think my mom or dad started it. It was your favorite or best part of your day, least favorite part of your day and the funniest part of your day. We'd go around the table and share and just recap the day. I remember that was always a tradition for us at family dinner. We had Sunday family dinners every week and we would always have those questions. We always had to have that ready. That was something that was fun.

ERIC BERMAN
CEO/FOUNDER *BRANDETIZE*

"

Yeah, it's interesting to get to know the real Brian. People see him on stage and they get a certain persona of Brian of being the professor, the teacher, the person who they worship for the teachings. They don't get an opportunity to really get to know Brian behind the scenes.

He's genuinely a fun, very loving, funny individual. We sit down with a bottle of red wine- it's his favorite- and have great dinners. We just talk everything in life from politics, to obviously a lot of business talk about experiences we've shared. We talk a lot about movies we like and TV shows. He's just very much like a father figure to me and it's great to get to know the fun personality side. He's a great guy."

CATHERINE TRACY
BRIAN'S DAUGHTER

"

It was definitely cool. I used to go into Barnes & Noble and be like, 'My dad writes books. Yeah, do you have Brian Tracy?' and they're like, 'Yeah, this is the section over here.' I'm like, 'That's my dad.'

I don't think he'll slow down. He's going to filter it down. He's never going to actually stop. Never. I don't think he'll ever actually stop speaking. He goes from 100 to 80 to 60 engagements a year. It's just going to be less and less. I don't think he'll ever stop."

BARBARA I think Brian feels that his life's mission is something that's still to be revealed to him, in addition to everything he's done. I don't think he thinks that what he's doing is the ultimate life mission. I, on the other hand, feel that what he has been doing for 30 years is his life's mission and that this life mission won't stop with him. It will be passed on with his books and tapes and seminars and the students he's had over time. It will be a continuously growing legacy.

7. PERSONAL FULFILLMENT & SELF-ACTUALIZATION

Scene: Speaking to audience

BRIAN

Number seven is personal fulfillment and self-actualization. Many people have asked me if the key to happiness in life is how much you like yourself, how much you love yourself, how much you love other people. How you feel about yourself determines your health, your happiness, your wealth. It determines the size of your goals. It determines how much you persist, how much you like yourself.

But what we have found is that you become what you think about most of the time, but you also become what you say to yourself most of the time. The transforming words that Barbara and I learned 35 years ago are the words, I like myself. I like myself. I like myself. I like myself. I like myself. I like myself. What we found when you first say those words, because of all the previous experiences in your life, is that you may feel a little uncomfortable, a little like, "Well, it's kind of cute and everything else." That's just telling you that you have some negative baggage back there that's blocking you, but the natural state of the human being is to like themselves unconditionally. Just to like themselves no matter what happens. Say the words:

I LIKE MYSELF.

"**THOSE ARE THE KEYS TO SUCCESS.**
AS LONG AS YOU HOLD ONTO THOSE WHENEVER YOU
HAVE A PROBLEM OR DIFFICULTY OF ANY KIND YOU GO
BACK TO THAT. I LIKE MYSELF AND I'M RESPONSIBLE. IF
THERE'S SOMETHING IN MY LIFE THAT'S NOT WORKING,
THEN BY GONE IT'S UP TO ME TO CHANGE IT. I'M NOT
GOING TO SIT HERE AND WHINE, MOAN AND CRY AND
WEEP AND BLAME OTHER PEOPLE. I JUST GET BUSY AND
DO SOMETHING ABOUT IT."